"A culmination of the writer's voice over the years: sincere and honest, heartfelt and meditative."   —KQED

"A swirling sea of sentiments, stories, and sounds. By the end, I am joyfully replenished."
—Luis J. Rodriguez, author of *Borrowed Bones*

"Mándanos luz, implores Sandra Cisneros, surrounded by suffering. 'Send us all light.' These poems do exactly that. They send us all light." —Martín Espada, author of *Floaters*

"Written with a vivid wild girl spirit, filled with unbridled love, angst, and joy!"
—Marilyn Chin, author of *Portrait of the Self as Nation*

"Inspirational in the best sense—reminding me yet again why poetry is so vital."
—Dorothy Allison, author of *Bastard Out of Carolina*

"*Woman Without Shame* dazzles with uninhibited energy."
—Rigoberto González, author of *The Book of Ruin*

"We are so lucky to have these brilliant poems."
—Jan Beatty, author of *American Bastard*

"Mahalo ā nui, Sista, for turning the satire of aging into vintage, rakish laughter, such a benevolent rarity."
—Lois-Ann Yamanaka, author of *Behold the Many*

Sandra Cisneros

Woman Without Shame

Sandra Cisneros was born in Chicago in 1954. Internationally acclaimed for her poetry and fiction, which has been translated into more than twenty-five languages, she is the recipient of numerous awards, including NEA Fellowships in both poetry and fiction, a MacArthur Fellowship, the Texas Medal of the Arts, the PEN/Nabokov Award for Achievement in International Literature, and the National Medal of Arts. She has fostered the careers of many aspiring and emerging writers through two nonprofits she founded: Macondo Writers, celebrating its twenty-seventh anniversary in 2022, and the Alfredo Cisneros del Moral Foundation, which operated for fifteen years. As a single woman, Cisneros made the choice to have books instead of children. Her literary papers are preserved at the Wittliff Collections at Texas State University. Currently she lives in San Miguel de Allende. Cisneros is a dual citizen of the United States and Mexico and earns her living by her pen.

sandracisneros.com

Woman

Without

Shame

Woman
Without
Shame

· Poems ·

SANDRA CISNEROS

VINTAGE BOOKS

A DIVISION OF PENGUIN RANDOM HOUSE LLC

NEW YORK

FIRST VINTAGE BOOKS EDITION 2023

Copyright © 2022 by Sandra Cisneros

All rights reserved. Published in the United States by Vintage Books,
a division of Penguin Random House LLC, New York, and distributed in Canada
by Penguin Random House Canada Limited, Toronto. Originally published in
hardcover in the United States by Alfred A. Knopf, a division of Penguin
Random House LLC, New York, in 2022.

Vintage and colophon are registered trademarks of Penguin Random House LLC.

Some poems originally appeared in the following publications: "Cielo sin sombrero
/ Sky Without a Hat," "Creed," and "Instructions for My Funeral" in *Black
Renaissance Noire;* "My Mother and Sex" and "Remedy for Social Overexposure"
in *North American Review;* "Smith's Supermarket, Taos, New Mexico, at the
Fifteen Items or Less Checkout Line" and "In My Little Museum of Erotica" in
Ploughshares; "It Occurs to Me I Am the Creative/Destructive Goddess Coatlicue"
in *The Massachusetts Review;* "Jarcería Shop" in *Nepantla Familias;* "I Should
Like to Fall in Love with a Burro Named Saturnino" and "This in the News
Unmentioned" in *Kenyon Review;* "You Better Not Put Me in a Poem," "A Boy with
a Machine Gun Waves to Me," and "Exploding Cigar of Love" in *Freeman's;* "Canto
for Women of a Certain Llanto," "El Hombre," and "God Breaks the Heart Again and
Again" in *Huizache;* "Día de los Muertos" in the *Los Angeles Times;* "Buen Árbol / A
Good Tree" in *Conjunctions;* "Our Father, Big Chief in Heaven" and "Never Mention
to the Daughters of the Republic of Texas" in *The Paris Review;* "Tea Dance,
Provincetown, 1982" in *The New Yorker;* "Having Recently Escaped from the Maws
of a Deathly Life, I Am Ready to Begin the Year Anew" and "Figs" in *Granta;* "After
a Quote from My Father," "When in Doubt," and "I Want to Be a Maguey in My Next
Life" in *Orion;* "K-Mart, San Antonio, Texas, 1986" in *Texas Monthly;* "In Case of
Emergency" and "Wasps in the Buddha Bell" in *Lion's Roar.* "El Hombre"
was commissioned by the Dallas Museum of Art.

The Library of Congress has cataloged the Knopf edition as follows:
Names: Cisneros, Sandra, author.
Title: Woman without shame: poems / Sandra Cisneros.
Description: First Edition. | New York: Alfred A. Knopf, 2022.
Identifiers: LCCN 2021048969 (print) | LCCN 2021048970 (ebook)
Subjects: LCGFT: Poetry.
Classification: LCC PS3553.I78 W67 2022 (print) | LCC PS3553.I78 (ebook) |
DDC 811/.54—dc23
LC record available at https://lccn.loc.gov/2021048969
LC ebook record available at https://lccn.loc.gov/2021048970

**Vintage Books Trade Paperback ISBN: 978-0-593-46811-1
eBook ISBN: 978-0-593-53483-0**

Book design by Pei Loi Koay

vintagebooks.com

Printed in the United States of America
1st Printing

for Norma Alarcón, poetry ally

CONTENTS

————◆————

Mujer sin vergüenza

Cantos y llantos

Cisneros sin censura

Pilón

Mujer

sin

vergüenza

———◆———

Tea Dance, Provincetown, 1982

At the boy bar, no
one
danced with me.

I danced with
every
one.

The entire
room.
Every song.

That's what was so
great
about the boy bars
then.

The room vibrated.
Shook.
Convulsed.

In one
collective
zoological
frenzy.

Truthfully,
I was the

only woman
there.

Who cared?
At the Boatslip,
I was welcomed.

The girl bar
down the street?
Pfft!
Dull as Brillo.

But the tea dances shimmied,
miraculous as mercury.
Acrid stink of sweat and
chlorine tang of semen.

Slippery male energy.
Something akin to
watching horses fighting.
Something exciting.

My lover,
the final summer he was bi,
introduced me to the teas.
Often hovered out of sight,
distracted by poolside
beauties, while I danced
content/innocent
with the room of men.

He was a skittish kite, that one.
Kites swerve and swoop and whoop.

Only a matter of time, I knew.
Apropos, I called him
"my little piece of string."
And that's what kites
leave you with in the end.

There was an expiration date
to summer. Understood.
That season,
I was experimenting to be
the woman I wanted to be.

Taught myself to sun
topless at the gay beach,
where sunbathers
shouted "ranger,"
a relayed warning
announcing authority,
en route on horseback,
coming to inspect
if we were clothed.
Else fined. Fifty
dollars sans bottom.
One hundred, topless.
Fifty a tit, I joked.

It was easy to be half naked
at a gay beach. Men
didn't bother to look.
I was in training to be
a woman without shame.

Not a shameless woman,
una sinvergüenza, but
una sin vergüenza
glorious in her skin.
Flesh akin to pride.
I shed that summer
not only bikini top but
guilt-driven Eve and
self-immolating Fatima.

Was practicing for
my Minoan days ahead.
Medusa hair and breasts
spectacular as Nike of Samothrace
welcoming the salty wind.
Yes, I was a lovely thing then.

I can say this with impunity.
At twenty-eight, she was a woman
unrelated to me. I could
tell stories. Have so many to tell
and none to tell them to
except the page.
My faithful confessor.

Lover and I feuded
one night when he
wouldn't come home with me.
His secret—herpes.
Laughable in retrospect,
considering the Plague
was already decimating dances
across the globe.

But that was before
we knew it as the Plague.

We were all on the run in '82.
Jumping to Laura Branigan's "Gloria,"
the summer's theme song.
Beat thumping in our blood.
Drinks sweeter than bodies
convulsing on the floor.

Creed

I believe I am God.
And you are too.
And each and everyone.
But only for a little.

I believe God is
Love, and love is God.
And although some
Doubt God's existence,
No one doubts the existence of love,
Even and especially those who have
Never met love.

I believe we are
Capable of atrocities beyond
Imagination and equally
Capable of extraordinary
God-acts as well.

I believe
There is enough misery
In the world, but also
Humanity—just a bit
More, I believe.

I believe in the power
Of a thought, a word,
To change the world.

I believe there is no greater
Sorrow than that of a mother
Who has lost her child.

I believe in *las madres,*
Las madres de las madres,
Y la santísima madre,
La diosa Guadalupe.

Because the universe is large enough
To encompass contradictions,
I believe these same mothers sometimes
Create monsters—*los machos.*

I believe mothers and grandmothers
Are the solution to violence,
Not only in Mexico / the United States,
But across the globe.

I believe what the generals need now
Are the *abuelita* brigades armed with
Chanclas to shame, swat, and spank
Los meros machos del mundo.
Amen.

At Fifty I Am Startled to Find I Am in My Splendor

These days I admit
I am wide as a *tule* tree.
My underwear protests.
And yet,

I like myself best
without clothes when
I can admire myself
as God made me, still
divine as a *maja*.
Wide as a fertility goddess,
though infertile. I am,
as they say,
in decline. Teeth
worn down, eyes burning
yellow. Of belly
bountiful and flesh
beneficent I am. I am
silvering in crags
of crotch and brow.
Amusing.

I am a spectator at my own sport.
I am Venetian, decaying splendidly.
Am magnificent beyond measure.
Lady Pompadour roses exploding
before death. Not old.

Correction, aged.
Passé? I am but vintage.

I am a woman of a delightful season.
El Cantarito, little brown jug of la Lotería.
Solid, stout, bottom planted
firmly and without a doubt,
filled to the brim I am.
I said the brim.

Remedy for Social Overexposure

Seek a *pirul* tree and sit
beneath immediately.
Remove from
ears and tongue,
words.
Fast from same.

Soak in a tub of seclusion.
Rinse face with wind.
In extreme cases, douse
oneself with sky. Then,
swab gently with clouds.

Dress in clean, pressed pajamas.
Preferably white.

Hold close to the heart,
chihuahuas. Kiss and
be kissed by same.

Consume a cool glass of night.
Read poetry that inspires poetry.
Write until temperament
returns to calm.

Place moonlight in a bowl.
Sleep beside and
dream of white flowers.

Never Mention to the Daughters
of the Republic of Texas

That you made love
on an office desk
on the seventeenth floor
with a view of the Alamo.

Saw it upside down.
Your head dangling
off the edge of the desk.
But saw it right for once.

Shook from memory—
Bosnia. How neighbor
upon neighbor fired.
Grief in one century
bred in another ire.
Reason collapsed
like Stari Most, a bridge
of five hundred years.

What do you know
of tears?

What you choose
to remember—
Beware.

K-Mart, San Antonio, Texas, 1986

FOR RUBÉN

When I can take you to the K-Mart
on South Santa Rosa at sunset,
and say, Meet me over by the flip-flops,
I've got to get me some socks.

When I can toss in the shopping cart
my tampons next to your Tres Flores
hair oil, my microwave popcorn, your
pack of white tees, my San Martín
de Porres three-day candle.

When we have finished paying
and can sit in the parking lot
satisfied, you and I,
with *nachos* and an Icee.

Then we can marvel
at a thousand black wings
swooping against the downtown sky.
Urracas urracando in the trembling trees.

Smith's Supermarket, Taos, New Mexico, at the Fifteen-Items-or-Less Checkout Line

The baby-faced *cholo* in front of me
gently drops a divider bar between
what's his and mine.

On my side, a six-outlet surge
protector for my computer,
and a fireproof glass cup
for my Lux Perpetua candle,
a votive so powerful
it self-destructs.

On his,
a plastic bottle of store-brand vodka.
It's noon, but somewhere
it's happy hour.

Baseball cap bad-ass backwards.
Black leather from neck to knees.
One brow and ear stitched with silver.
And on his neck, "Rufina" in wispy
ink I would kiss if I could. Fool,
it takes one to know one.

I drive away wondering
if Rufina is helping him
drink his bottle of forget.
Or if it's she who is regret.

I write till the dark descends.
My cell warm tonight.
Candles. *Copal.*
Outside my window,
mountain without a moon.
Buddha in lotus.
Silent and still.

By ten, hot bath, lavender salts.
Flannel buttoned to the neck.
Am certain Rufina is not
as happy as I am tonight,
in bed with my love,
a book.

Noche, La Casa Magdalena, Lamy, New Mexico

FOR SUSAN AND BERT

i.

All night,
wind rattles
at my door
like an over-
sexed lover
wanting in.

ii.

Yellow
flowers
in your
Guada-
lupe
nicho
remem-
ber when
they were
wild.

Tired,
they furl

themselves
  to sleep.

...

iii.

A *borracho*
  slings a beer
bottle against
  the sky.

One billion
  trillion
stars.

After a Quote from My Father

FOR LEVI ROMERO

The floors are sticky
With golden leaves
The dogs and I track in
On the soles of our feet.

Winter clothes need
To be brought down.
Make the bed.
Comb hair.
Wash the body.
Sleep.

Too many to-do's
Posted on
My nose.

Check bank balance.
Stop at vet.
Pick up spray
For fleas.

None say:

Look at the moon.
Write poetry.
Take *you* time, *mija*.
Take *you* time.

Wasps in the Buddha Bell

Must be deaf
or devout on
this A. A.

Milne–blustery day.
On this wind-like-a-
bugle Emily day.

Deaf or devout,
they neither
desert

their monastery
nor appear
enraged.

Bell gongs.
And they
pray.

Ommmmmm.
Ommmmmm.
Ommmmmm.

Calendar in the Season of the Pandemic

the ants have
deserted
my shower
for the garden

at long last
spring

In Case of Emergency

Contact nearest
cloud. Begin by
calling Milky Way.

Summon:
pepper tree,
maguey,
donkey shit,
jacaranda shower,
river,
caliche,
scorpion,
hummingbird,
or pearl.

Will vouch
we are
kin.

Instructions for My Funeral *

For good measure,
smoke me with *copal*.
Shroud me in my raggedy *rebozo*.
No jewelry. Give to friends.
No coffin. Instead, *petate*.
Ignite to "Disco Inferno."

Allow no Christian rituals
for this bitch, but, if
you like, you may invite
a homeless dog to sing,
or a witch woman to spit
orange water and chant
an Otomí prayer.

Send no ashes north
of the Río Bravo
on penalty of curse.

I belong here,
under Mexican *maguey*,
beneath a carved mesquite
bench that says *Ni Modo*.

Smoke a Havana.
Music, Fellini-esque.
Above all,
laugh.

And don't
forget.

Spell
my name
with *mezcal.*

* With acknowledgment to Javier Zamora and his poem of the same
title, though we each wrote our poems at about the same time,
perhaps at the same moment, without having read one another's.
Saint Coincidence, as Joy Harjo would say.

It Occurs to Me I Am the Creative/ Destructive Goddess Coatlicue

I deserve stones.
Better leave me the hell alone.

I am besieged.
I cannot feed you.
You may not souvenir my bones,
knock on my door, camp, come in,
telephone, take my polaroid. I'm paranoid,
I tell you. *Lárguense.* Scram.
Go home.

I am anomaly. Rare she who
can't stand kids and can't stand you.
No excellent Cordelia cordiality have I.
No coffee served in tidy cups.
No groceries in the house.

I sleep to excess,
smoke cigars,
drink. Am at my best
wandering undressed,
my fingernails dirty,
my hair a mess.
Terribly

sorry, Madame isn't
feeling well today.
Must

Greta Garbo.
Pull an Emily:
"The soul selects her own society . . ."
Roil like Rhys's Sargasso Sea.
Abiquiu à la O'Keeffe.
Throw a Maria Callas.
Shut myself like a shoe.

Christ
almighty. Stand
back. Warning.
Honey,
this means
you.

Cielo

sin

sombrero

———

Cielo con sombrero

El cielo amaneció
con su propio sombrero
hecho de lana
sucia de borrego.

Un sombrero tan ancho
que deja la tierra en sombras
teñida de añil y lavanda.

Como el mar
visto desde una isla
de cara a tierra firme.

Como los trastes de peltre
de los campesinos
que comen sin cuchara.

Sky Wearing a Hat

Sky arose
with a hat all its own
made from dirty
sheep-wool.

A hat wide
enough to dye the earth
indigo and lavender with shade.

Like sea
seen from an island
facing land.

Like the pewter dishes
of country folk
who eat without spoons.

Jarcería Shop *

A breakfast tray please. For my terrace.
In the morning I invite the bees
To raisin bread with lavender honey.
Don't worry, there's always
Enough for everybody.

I'll take a few of those *carrizo*
Baskets, strong enough for a woman
To haul a kilo of fresh oranges
From the Ignacio Ramírez market.
As if. I usually send Calixto,
The handyman.

Add a palm fan.
And an *ocote* stick or two.
For the fire I'll never ignite.
Solo de adorno, of course.
To amuse spirit ancestors!

Can you bring down
That papier-mâché doll?
Dressed in her best underwear.
I had one just like it as a girl.
No, I don't have kids.

A *comal* would be nice
To reheat my evening *tamal*.

Only a *comal* gives it
That smoky flavor.
I don't know how
To make *tamales*.
Why bother when
You can buy them
From the nuns.

A *molcajete*? Maybe.
Would make a cool bird
Bath for my yard.

Ay, and *ixtle*—
Maguey fibers
Hairy and white as
The grandfather's chest—
To strop the skin raw in the shower.

My outdoor sink,
With ribs like a hungry dog's,
Could use a step-stool stone
That dances *un danzón*,
And an *escobeta* scrub brush
Cinched tight at the waist
Like a ballerina.

Please deliver a fresh *petate*
With its palm tree scent
For my bedroom floor.
In the old days they were
My ancestors' coffins.

And that ball of *mecate* string.
Might as well.

Plus a lidded straw basket
To store plastic market bags
The colors of the Mexican
Tianguis—

Sky turquoise,
Geranium coral,
Jacaranda, amethyst,
Tender green of
Fresh *nopal* paddles.

A cotton hammock
Wide as a market woman,
So while I sleep
The pepper tree can bless me.

Six *carrizo* poles
To hang the new curtains
Made from *coyuchi* cotton.

I came for a cage
For my onyx parrot—
A goodbye gift from my agent
Attached with a warning.
Don't move south.

Los abuelos,
Who couldn't read, fled
North during the revolution,

With only what
They could carry in *un rebozo.*

And here I am at fifty-eight
Migrating in the opposite direction
With a truck hauling my library.

I live *al revés,* upside down.
Always have.
Who called me here? Spirits maybe.
A century later. To die at home for them
Since they couldn't.

And for my cobbled courtyard,
Your best branch broom
With a fine *shh-shh,*
Like the workers who sweep up
Saturday night on Sunday
Morning in el Jardín.

And, a bucket.
To fill with suds.
For the simple glory of scrubbing
Mexican porch tiles
In my bare brown feet.

When I feel like it.
On the housekeeper's day off.

To set the grandmothers
Grinding their gravestone teeth.

*This from the *Diccionario de la Real Academia Española* (*The Dictionary of the Royal Spanish Academy*):

jarcería
f. Méx. Shop where objects made from vegetable fibers are sold. An archaic word, hardly in use anymore.

El Jardín, End of Day

To lose a kilo I walk
round and round el Jardín.

A monk hunkered in grief
is praying, I think.

Till I reel past his park bench
and note his book of hours.
His iPhone.

Under *los portales,*
a Mexican boy kisses
a boney *gringuita.*

No doubt he sees her
with Mexican eyes.
Bellísima
because she's blond.

But *los norteamericanos*
see her with American eyes.
Nothing to write home about.

I imagine she sees him
with *turista* eyes.
Aztec beautiful.

But *mexicanos*
see him as *feo*
because he's *indio*.

Night hovers.
Tourists lick ice cream cones
before setting out to dinner.

Kids in a sugar fury bounce
inflatable rockets on
church flagstones.

Beer bottles belch open.
Twilight sticky with the fried
scent of burgers and tacos.

Tethered to owners,
little dogs sniff concrete.
The cathedral an apricot hue,
sunburnt as *los extranjeros*.

Flocks of *mariachi* descend
itchy for work.

Balloon seller fidgets,
adjusts his yoke of
balloons and blow-up toys.
Shoulder aches.
Even air must weigh something.

While the sweets vendor
floats across the plaza
with a tree of cotton candy
the same colors as clouds.

I Should Like to Fall in Love with a Burro Named Saturnino

I should like to fall in love
with a burro named Saturnino
and sleep murmuring
that name as lullaby.

Warm my bed
with a *xoloitzcuintli*
the color of blue corn,
and will myself to be reborn
sunflower, ever
faithful to the sun.

I should like to learn to love
with the monogamous
passion of the parrot
and the foolish
valor of the *chihuahua*.

I should love to dedicate
my morning glory years
to the inspirational ants, who
peacefully and, without remorse
or humor, successfully evict me
from my shower every winter,
lessons in nonviolent persuasion.

I have much to learn from
the sentinel *maguey* about
fortitude, resilience, patience
in this season of *los santos
inocentes de la política.*

And day by day I am a student
of the morning sky.
And night by night I memorize
the sermon of the guru moon.

Next to my door
there is an *ixtle* rope
attached to a bronze bell
announcing visitors.

It does not ring when dawn arrives
with her furious scent of *bolillos,*
orange peels, and doorways
flushing buckets of Fabuloso
across wet stone.

Every day the same as the one before.
And never as the one before. Each moment
wrapped in newsprint and twine
and delivered always on time.

Figs

FOR DR. BRUNO CEOLIN

Some words
trip me
in my second tongue.

I say
pepino—cucumber
when I mean
pimienta—pepper.

Confuse
ginebra—gin,
when I mean
ginger—*jengibre*.

And when
the acupuncturist
tells me—
El hígado enamorado
quiere decir
el cuerpo está sano.
The liver in love
means the body is healthy—

I mistake
hígado—liver,
for fig—*higo*.

I prefer my translation.

All's right with the world
when figs are in love.

Neither Señorita nor Señora

I didn't love
those who did.

And did
those who didn't.

Once
I almost proposed
in Paris.

Because it was Paris!
My heart
Fragonard's shoe.

But he was afraid
of the Pont Neuf
and lingering
in the rain.

Another, too
busy saving worlds
to think of saving us,
I press between
the pages of my thighs.

Tender green
lost me to the darkness

under trees. And
lost himself to drink.

Worst,
the pest who could not love
at all, whom I loved best.
Shame!

I wanted as souvenir—
cue the violins please—
his child.

Even if disastrous
for the kid
and my career.

But that's history.

More recently,
an exploding cigar.
Need I say more?

God saves fools
too foolish to
save themselves.

And now,
the Orizaba
years.

Here I have
no answer how
I got from then to now.

Except,
with gratitude
to all,
I bow.

Our Father, Big Chief in Heaven

Our Father,
big chief in heaven,
I sent my assistant Calixto
to make an appointment
with Her Highness, *la licenciada,*
who has left for lunch before noon,
gone for the day, was fired, or fled,
who can tell; the third director
at this post in fifteen months.

Deliver us
from the bearded tenor
who schedules at said institution,
busy today trimming his whiskers—
"My will be done. Thy kingdom come . . .
back tomorrow."

Forgive us
our trespasses, as
we forgive *el notario,*
who ought to be called el Notorious,
for having us wait three months
for his return call, so Calixto and wife
can finally sign the deed on their first
home, having given up on the
call from their own *notario,* even
slower than mine, and already
waiting weary.

Everything
on earth is done
with *papeles,* signatures, patience,
and the arrival of others, whose
destiny is out of our hands, especially
if you are a native in this native land.

Father,
I know we
should be grateful for our small pains
in a nation where it's easier to break
than follow law, where widows grieve
without recompense or consolation,
where limbs and heads of journalists
are delivered in trash bags when
they dare to print the truth,
where dogs bite with impunity,
masons fall from scaffolds in a puff
of dust and broken bones,
if lucky.

Eternally glad are we for our small woes.
Blessed are we to bed with all our appendages.
Bless our winged tenor and *la licenciada chiflada,*
our future on their whims depends.
Blessed be especially our Notorious; one day
may he yet sign our documents.
Give us this day our plentitude of wait.
And praise our politicians,
who teach us daily to endure.

Stretch our hearts ample as a yawn,
so we might accommodate the double-
wide trailer of our neighbors' grief,
and, by comparison, feel
gratitude for our own. Misery
without end. Amen.

This in the News Unmentioned

The aged seamstress on
The old road to Querétaro
Has no work. Her
Sewing machine is broken.
Her eyes as well.

The rose seller from Santa Julia
Reads Neruda and dreams
Of buying his mother a stove.
It is the time of rain. She
Cooks outdoors with firewood.

The housekeeper's five
Sons have all gone north.
Her favorite won't phone, and
She can neither read nor write.

Meanwhile, arms drift south
And drugs shift north.
The avocados, beyond the budget
Of the seamstress, rose seller,
Housekeeper, travel north too
This season.

Police. Politicians.
México. United States.
Business always good
Between the two
Nations.

El Hombre

AFTER TAMAYO

On the eve of International Women's Day
In a field on the road to Celaya
They find her body.
The deaf-mute girl who
Walked her dog in Parque Juárez.

No one tried, blamed, named.
The town knows:

It's her father's debts.
This is how they pay
Un hombre who can't pay.

Mándanos luz. Send us all light.

In small print, in the back
Pages of today's paper,
I read this small news:

Un Hombre Purépecha
Lifted from His Purépecha Village.

Daily the Purépechas demand his return.
Daily *el hombre* does not return.

He is only one of the many "lifted."

When you are native in your native land
To whom do you demand? Who listens?

Mándanos luz. Send us all light.

The bird merchant at the Tuesday *mercado*,
Six cages of *cenzontles* strapped on his back,
Shoves a mesh shopping bag so close
To my face, I have to step back to see.
A flutter of frightened canaries.
In the eyes of *el hombre*,
The same urgency, the same fear.

Mándanos luz. Send us all light.

The *gringo* Alan tells me the story
Of the pig who thought he was a dog.
Solovino he was called,
Because he came alone.

How each day Alan drove
Along the road to Dolores,
The dogs would run from
The squatter's shack and give chase,
The pig who thought he was a dog
Trotting behind them.

Until one day the pig isn't there.
The dogs disappear too.
One by one by one.

Alan shrugs.
When *un hombre* is hungry,
There is no one to blame.

Mándanos luz. Send us all light.

The "Religion" section of
Our Guanajuato newspaper
Features an article on St. Francis,
Un hombre of austerity, as
A model for all to live in poverty.

This in a country where almost every
Hombre, mujer y niño is already
On the path to sainthood.

Mándanos luz. Send us all light.

How it happened was like this.
One night Rosana catches *un hombre*
Breaking into her grocery store,
The son of a neighbor.

Her shouts wake the *barrio*.
They're able to hold the thief
Until the police arrive.

Rosana is there to bear witness
At the court proceedings. And to
Witness the court set him free.

She gathers her pain in a handkerchief,
Goes home and calls the boy's mother.

Rosana and the mother of the thief. Each
Woman lets loose a sea of grief.

When she tells me this story,
The sea is still there in Rosana's eyes.

Mándanos luz. Send us all light.

Carlos and Raúl, the silver-tongued
Poets of Chicano, Illinois, have never
Been to the country of their ancestry,
Though they're silver-haired *hombres*.

When I invite them south, they refuse.
They're afraid of bad *hombres*.

No one has told them
The ones who buy drugs and

Sell arms to *los* bad *hombres*
Are U.S. citizens.

Mándanos luz. Send us all light.

The blind harmonica player,
Un hombre who plays "Camino de Guanajuato"
In front of Banco Santander,
Clutches his baseball cap of small coins
Whenever he hears someone running too close.

No vale nada la vida, la vida no vale nada.
Life's worth nothing, nothing is what life's worth.

Mándanos luz. Send us all light.

Un hombre tells me:
You don't even have to learn Spanish to live here.
Amado the San Miguel realtor.
You can train your staff to do what you need,
And you don't have to pay them much either.

Mándanos luz. Send us all light.

Dallas, 1953.
A seer named Stanley Marcus

Purchases a mural by Rufino Tamayo
To reinforce friendship between
Texas and Mexico.

This in a time in history
When Texas still posts
Signs on restaurants:
"No dogs or Mexicans."

The painting is of *un hombre*
Anchored to the earth
Reaching for the heavens,
A balance of earth and sky,
North and south, yours and mine.
Because the universe is
About interconnection.

Tamayo calls this painting,
Man Excelling Himself.

Mándanos luz. Send us all light.

Message from Mexico to
The United States of America:
When we are safe, you are safe.
When you are safe, we are safe.
Tell this to your politicians.

Mándanos luz. Send us all light.

There is a Mexican saying,
Hablando se entiende la gente.
Talking to one another
We understand one another.

I would add: And listening
We understand even better.

Mándanos luz. Send us all light.
Mándanos luz. Send us all light.
Mándanos luz. Send us all light.

Adelina Cerritos

Adelina Cerritos,
at your service. Thin
shrug and a *ni modo* grin.

Could you
use some help *quizás*?

Might you
need a cook perhaps?

Maybe someone
to do the wash?

Brings her knuckles together
in a scrub woman's prayer.

Adelina of the nubby
sweater and plastic shoes.
Adelina of the pewter hair.

It's that I have a medical
appointment in Celaya
and not enough *pesos*
to get there.

It's that my breasts are
charred from the chemo.
Chamuscados, she says.

Charred. *Tortillas*
forgotten on the *comal*.

Adelina *del campo*.
Adelina *de* Guanajuato. Thin
shrug and a *ni modo* grin.

Te A—

A boy and a girl embrace, kiss
within the triangle of my parking
space. A geometric equation
proving the whole greater
than the sum of the parts.
Beyond the eye of Church,
traffic, and mothers, here,
in the privacy of a *callejón*
that rolls soundlessly downhill,
dissolves into the wall of
the chapel of San Juan de Dios,
patron of booksellers, alcoholics,
and the sick, sufferers all . . .
Even in a town
named for an armed angel,
love finds a route.
        A boy and a girl kiss:
seven mute organ cacti
and a *nicho de* Guadalupe
as witnesses.

To prove love is ever
expanding in space and time,
the boy drafts a Valentine
on the parking triangle's
hypotenuse—
my neighbor's stone wall.
        "Te" . . .

sprayed red in block letters.
       Then "A" . . .

Across town,
as *narcos* duly collect protection
rent from *tortilla* vendors,
even as townsfolk disappear,
like wallets plucked from
Costco customers' pockets,
and lifetime savings are obediently
stashed at bus stop trash bins
per phone extortionists' instruction,
while gentle twilight descends,
releasing, soundless as moths,
serial rapists,
the authorities move swiftly
when children violate
property owned by foreigners.
Love, after all,
is a dangerous conflagration,
an axiom even
Euclid would conclude.

The boy is let go with a few
slaps for his proper education.
The girl wisely escaped at the first
sight of uniforms and guns.

And so, as it was before,
and ever will be,
the neighbor's wall is
power-hosed to its former

serenity. Except
for a faint pink scar:

Te A—
    Te A—

A song crowned with
humility and thorns,
extending into infinity,
stigmata of the forlorn.

A Boy with a Machine Gun Waves to Me

Maybe he is the same
age as the forty-three
from Ayotzinapa,
burned and buried
like trash.

Dark of skin perhaps
the same as the Atotonilco
man arrested and jailed
after a gunfire exchange
he did not begin,
in front of his own,
in front of his home.

Or in collusion with those
who abducted the blind
girl from Parque Juárez
and abandoned her shell
on the road to Celaya,
wrapped in a blanket,
forever in a field of sleep.

He's in the back of a jeep
with other boys. They
could be a baseball team.
Instead, they're dressed
in black uniforms,

on their way to work
with machine guns.

I was coming from the market
with a basket of eggs
and a round loaf of bread,
a *xoloitzcuincli* perched
warm in the crook of my arm.

By Callejón de los Muertos,
their jeep rumbled past.
So many sons armed
with guns like toys,
though I know they're
real because I've asked.

Before they disappear
from view, my hand
raises itself as if
asking a question.

From the back of the jeep
a hand without a machine gun
answers back.

Tepoztlán

roosters
yodel

dogs
debate

church bells
hiccup

dawn
yawns

Señor Martín

First, the urgent story
about an operation
for his lung. For sympathy,
he posed as mute and wrote
his plea on wrinkled paper.

Doubtful. All the same,
I gave. He was not young.
I lowered my donation
from the balcony
in a mesh market bag
on *ixtle* rope.

On his next call,
I offered to organize
a collection if he would
leave hospital details
in my mailbox.
But he forgot.

His lung was cured
by the next week.
His voice as well,
miraculously
restored.

Then he came
with only his unnamed
need and no story.

I had no change
except five hundred pesos,
which the bank machines
dispense like PEZ
to *extranjeros* like me.

Hard to find anyone,
humble or lordly, willing to
part ways with smaller currency.
I gave him what I had then.
Five hundred pesos, but
this brought him back
swifter than a swallow.
Sometimes twice
within a week,
enough to raise my ire
and blow my Buddhahood.

Back and back again he came.
Calixto said he knows him
as Martín, who leads the
donkey for the wedding
callejoneadas.

He looks like no party
host to me. Scraggy
as a cat. Thin mustache,
the kind pranksters
add on the *Mona Lisa.*
Dirty newsboy cap.
Glass shards for eyes.
Clothes borrowed, perhaps.

A Chekhov peasant, not
pandemic-unemployed. Or,
maybe victim of his own
vices. Who knows?

Sometimes he raises hell
when I refuse to answer,
ringing my brass bell
like the San Juan de Dios church
calling forth the faithful.
As if the schoolhouse is on fire.

I gave him once
one hundred pesos.
Then one weekend I had
no change at all but fifty.
He seemed to agree on this price.

Now he nods in gratitude,
and I apologize for sending
him running after money
when the wind has fun.

Saturdays,
or sometimes Sundays,
when he knows Calixto isn't
here, he comes.

And so, with time
this is how we've settled
on what's fair.
I can imagine how

hard it is to be him,
how hard to ask.

Today I sent him
with his weekly share.
Surprised him.
Surprised myself
by saying
for the first time—
"Cuídese, Señor Martín."

Swallows, Guanajuato Airport

At home in the "o"
of GUANAJUATO,
golondrinas.

Cielo sin sombrero

Voy a vender
el cielo San Miguelense,
este azul jacaranda
que queda tan bonito
junto a los techos de barro.

Seguro que está a la venta.
Por supuesto que sí.
Ya que aquí
Se Vende,
Se Alquila,
Se Renta
todo.

Monte,
memoria,
río,
mujer,
historia,
ajonjolí.

El cielo lo venderé
a rebanadas.
Y a los extranjeros
les cobraré el doble
por doblar
el costo de la vida.

¡Atención!
Se vende un cielo sin sombra,
este cielo celeste al que tanto
le hace falta un sombrero.

Y,
si me inspiro
y me va bien,

Alquilo Nubes
también.

Sky Without a Hat

I'm going to sell
the San Miguel sky,
this *jacaranda* blue
that suits perfectly
clay roofs.

Of course, it's available.
Absolutely and for sure.
Here everything is
For
Sale,
Rent,
Lease.

Mountain,
prickly pear,
hacienda,
stone,
woman,
mud.

I'll sell sky
by the slice.
Charge foreigners
double
for doubling
the cost of living.

Attention!
Sky without shade
for sale, this celestial
blue in bad need
of a hat.

And,
if all goes
as planned:

Clouds
For Rent.

Police Blotter, May 5th, 2013, San Miguel de Allende

Piropos given to the elderly—one.

Listening without interrupting—four.

Admiration for wildlife without intent to kill—two.

Homes on Sunday with no one knocking on the door—seven.

Hugging and kissing babies—one hundred and eleven.

Vehicles loaned to the needy—three.

Pedestrians halted by *jacaranda*—thirteen.

Employees who love their jobs—eight.

Healed by laughter—sixty-seven.

Domestic harmony—thirty-three.

Citizens held hostage by the sunset—fifty-six.

Beautification and creation in lieu of violence—twenty-one.

Orderly conduct without force—forty-four.

Gifts of money with no personal motive—five.

Telephone kindness—thirteen.

Sexual generosity—three.

Poems delivered—one.

Quiero ser maguey en mi próxima vida

Dar cara al sol todo el día.
Reventar hijos al aire
Como una piñata.

Ahorrar agua.
Brotar una flor con fleco estirándose al cielo.
Estirando, estirando al cielo, qué lujo.

Quiero pertenecer a estas tierras
Que existían antes de que
El mundo fuera redondo.

Picar las nalgas
De los que se acercan demasiado.
Regalar aguamiel al que se atreve a
Chupar mi jugo.

Y morir de esta comunión.
Deshacerme como ceniza.
Volver a vivir en la tierra.

Violenta.
Explotar de la huerta como Paricutín.
Volver volver volver a renacer.
Morir para siempre ser.

I Want to Be a Maguey in My Next Life

Face to the sun all day.
Burst offspring into the air
Like a *piñata*.

Store water.
Bloom a tasseled flower
Stretching itself to the sky.
Stretching, stretching to the sky,
What luxury.

I want to belong to these lands
That existed before the world
Was round.

Pinch the asses of those who
Come too close to me.
Give *aguamiel* to the one who dares
Suck my juice.

And die from this communion.
Dissolve like ash.
Return to live on earth.

Violent.
Detonate from a field like Paricutín.
Return return return to be reborn.
Die to eternally be.

Cantos

y

llantos

———

Back Then or Even Now

A SONG FOR GUITAR

I liked being young
with you once.
A moment or two,
here and there
with you once.

When you
were a poet,
and I was a poet.
Wordsmiths afraid
of the words
shimmering
right before us.

I remember censoring
myself when I was sober.
Spontaneous combustion
when I wasn't.

We did a lot of things
back then
under the courage
of alcohol.

We were a two-
ring-circus knife act.
Blade zinging

in the air, thud-
landing near
a shivering artery.
A thrill, a chill a minute.
Me and you.

I was leaving town,
and you were staying.
That's why we each held
back from saying.

It takes growing older
to see some things
imagined were real.
Back then or even now.

Canto for Women of a Certain Llanto

AFTER DYLAN THOMAS

I'd rather wear none
than ugly underwear made
for women of a certain age.

Rage, rage. Do not go into that good night
wearing sensible white or beige.

Women who have squash-
blossomed into soft flesh,
and grieve the frothy loss of the interior
garments of youth.

Rage, rage. Do not go into that good night
wearing sensible white or beige.

Gone the black-lace architecture of the past,
the thong, bikinis, hipsters, G-strings. Gone, gone.

The underwire and lace push-up cups
replaced with feed sacks and ace
bandage straps. Pachydermian.
Prosthetic. A cruel aesthetics.

Rage, rage. Do not go into that good night
wearing sensible white or beige.

Excellent women, who in wise vision flower,
blaze, scintillate in your finest era.
Refuse the misnomer "Intimate Apparel."
For what lies beyond XL or 36C is
the antithesis of intimacy.
Garments sent to exile *ánimas solas*
to the Siberia of celibacy.
To sleep with dogs or cats
instead of lovers.

Oh, La Perla, why hast thou forsaken us?
Will no one take pity and design foundations, nay,
lingerie for women of exuberance?
Something imaginative,
like Frank Lloyd Wright's Fallingwater.

In my imagination I create a holster
to pack my twin firearms. My 38-38's.
A beautiful invention of oiled
Italian leather graced tobacco golden,
whip-stitched, hand-tooled
with Western roses and winged scrolls,
mother-of-pearl snaps
and nipples capped with silver aureoles.

And you, my mother,
gazing from your *chaparrita* height,
who has cursed and blessed
me with your DNA like so many
Mexican women with a pillar for a torso
like Coatlicue.

Magas, brujas, chingonas.
Rage, rage. Do not go into that good night
wearing sensible white or beige.

Washing My Rebozo by Hand

I wash my silk *rebozo* in the shower
against my naked skin
to keep the fringe from knotting.
Fuchsia cloth draped over my shoulder,
one Amazon breast exposed.

Even folded in half, the shawl
is longer than I am tall,
fringe work grazing the floor.

For an instant, the water
spills out hot as August
when I turn on the tap,
and I regret my reckless idea
to wash the cloth myself.
Bougainvillea darkens to cranberry,
but, thankfully, the color doesn't run.
Fibers slick as corn silk when rinsed.

The wet *rebozo* conforms to my skin
like dough draped over my *empanada* belly,
eggplant breasts, Coatlicue ass.
I admire myself in the mirror.
Some ancient memory approves.

And I think of that fool William Frawley,
of *I Love Lucy,* who said of co-star Vivian Vance,
"She has a body like a sack of doorknobs."

At fifty-six
my Buddha body
bows to gravity.
A life lived.

I am not a sack of doorknobs.

At these heights,
I like myself enough to pose
in this poem just as I am,
solid as Teotihuacán.

A woman of an age
she doesn't give a damn

what's said
by a sack of *pitos*
posing as a man.

Having Recently Escaped from the Maws of a Deathly Life, I Am Ready to Begin the Year Anew

For the New Year I will buy myself a chocolate éclair filled with custard. Eat it slowly, with an infinity of joy, without concern of woe and tight underwear.

Susan's mother was directed by her doctor to cut down on salami or risk death. "But, doctor," she said, "is life worth living without salami?"

For my new year I will sit down in the sun and dunk in my coffee a little knob of bread hard as my elbow, and on it, without concern for cholesterol, I will spread delicious butter, the kind that reminds me of Mexico City's Café La Blanca on Calle Cinco de Mayo, or the clinking glasses of El Gran Café de la Parroquia in Veracruz.

I will snooze with my dogs till I radiate love, for they are life's true gurus. I will wake gently so as not to disturb the dreams that have alighted overnight on the branches of sleep, and before they flutter away on soundless wings, I will examine and admire each.

This season of my escape, I will push my foot down on the accelerator of my life, *vámonos vobiscum,* and hurry to sit under a tree with a book thicker than a dozen homemade *tamales.* Henceforth, I will read only for pleasure or transmogrification.

All toxic folk are to be excised from the remaining days of my life, the *chupacabras* and *chupacabronas,* who are a purgatory of pain.

I will allow myself the luxury to laugh daily and in liberal doses to overbalance the bitter compost called the news.

I will cease waiting for someone to do something about the war, the walls, the guns, the drugs, the stupidity of leaders, and ally myself with citizens who practice the art of tossing their shoes at heads of state.

There is much I know and much I do not know as a woman at fifty-six, but I am certain I know this. Life is not worth living without salami.

Four Poems on Aging

Ménière's

This loss of the
Right ear's hearing,
No cross.

I only half listen
Anyhow.

Funny Bone

So much depends
Upon a staircase
Glazed with
Rainwater
Seven
Years
Ago.

A Universal Truth

Expanding
Like the universe:
Teats, ass, feets.

Floaters

FOR DR. JULIE TSAI

They taunt and tease
        From peripheral vision.

Duendes at quiet play.
        Semi-colons too

Coy to see directly.
        Dr. Tsai my opthamologist

Insists:
        "Harmless. I've checked."

To date, three
        Medals of distinction.

One on my right.
        Two on the left.

Both dizzy as cinder.
        Startling like falling leaves.

"Harmless," she says.
        I say, I'll believe it

When I see it.

Making Love After Celibacy

I bled a little,
Like the first time.
There was pain.

Not unlike the first time.
And a winged bliss
Just beyond reach.

Like that first time, too.
More pain than rhapsody.
To be sure.

A female body
Ashamed of itself again.
Not a girl's modesty

This time.
A woman's apology for
Erosion and weather.

The body offered
Like an altar
Of *xempoaxóchitl* marigolds.

A poor woman's offering
Of maize and water.
An offering all the same.

Lullaby

The world
turns
in the same
direction
that I do
as I sleep.

I turn
and help,
in turn,
the planet
turn.

The planet
turns.
And
gently
turns me
in my sleep.

Instructions for Vigiling the Dying

1. Take notes.

2. Cut a lock of hair.

3. Say what you feel and
   say it with conviction.
   Even if she can't hear.

4. Forgive.
   Especially yourself.

5. Tell her she can go.

6. Give yourself permission to let her go.

7. Give yourself permission to cry.
   If not now, when?

8. Hold her hand.

9. Pay attention to how the face transmogrifies.
   Especially the nose and ears.

10. Imagine you are the moon.
    Bathe yourself with light.
    Bathe the dying.
    Gently. With care.

11. Breathe.

12. Focus on this moment.

13. Grieve.

14. There are no rules.
    Not even these.

Exploding Cigar of Love

TO THE TUNE OF EL "HOKEY POKEY"

You toss your *corazón* in.
I toss my *corazón* in.
We toss our *corazones* together,
And we shake them all about.
We light the love cigar,
And we get a little high.
And that's what it's all about.

I write a poem for you.
You write a love poem—*for me?*
We send a hundred and three emails,
And we shake them all about.
We light the love cigar,
And we get a little high.
And that's what it's all about.

You advance *un paso.*
I retreat *pa'trás.*
I *tacuachito* toward you,
And you take a two-step back.
The more I pull, the more you tug.
The more you push, the more I scram.
What are we?
Pepé Le Pew and the cat?

You toss in sub self-esteem.
I toss in emotional hemophilia.

Insecurities, addictions,
And we mix them all about.
We light the love cigar,
And we get a little high.
And that's what it's all about.

You text: You're too much for me, baby.
I text: Well, maybe you're not enough!
You text: I need to be free.
And I'm shakin' all about.
We've been tripping on the love cigar.
Now sobriety sets in. Bang!
And that's what it's all about.

God Breaks the Heart Again and Again
Until It Stays Open

AFTER A QUOTE FROM SUFI INAYAT KHAN

But what if my heart is a 7-Eleven after its third daytime robbery in a week?

What if my heart is a *piñata* trashed to tissue and peppermint shrapnel?

What if my heart is a peeled mango bearing an emerald housefly?

What if my heart is an air conditioner weeping a rosary of rusty tears?

What if my heart is Sebastião Salgado's sinkhole swallowing another child?

What if my heart is Death Valley in wide-view Cinemascope?

What if my heart is a *chupacabrón* chanting, "Build the wall!"?

What if my heart is the creepy uncle's yawning zipper?

What if my heart is a Pentecostal babbling a river of tongues?

What if my heart is the cross-eyed Jesus bought at the Poteet flea market?

What if my heart is El Paso, Texas, in bed with the corpse of Ciudad Juárez?

What if my heart is unhinged from the weight of its lice-ridden wings?

What then for an encore, oh my soul, when you have blessed me a hundredfold?

Mrs. Gandhi

When Gandhi took his vow of celibacy, did he consult first with Mrs. Gandhi? Or simply take his path gradually and silently? So she would not protest. Peacefully or violently.

Wise it might've been to not seek dialogue with her. His work was worry enough. Mrs. Gandhi attributed to this his gradual nocturne apathy.

Complain? He went about his own tasks selflessly. How could she take offense? How could she blame? A pain as private and perfect as a river stone. She consigned grief to a sandalwood chest alongside doubts.

Maybe the abandonment was abrupt. Overnight. A sudden insult to her age. A small rage lingering that made her chastise herself as vain. Or did she simply bow and go, so to speak, with the Ganges?

Did Gandhi's kids complain daddy was away—again!—on his campaigns? Did sons resent father and father sons? Did wife wish she were again the far-away wife? She knew too well how sometimes it is lonelier with company than with solitude.

When Gandhi took his vow of celibacy, were temptations too many, and so he declared, *This drama is too time consuming.* An itch he wished to remove before the scratch. He reasoned the body was to be abandoned eventually, so taught the Hindus. Why not walk away now, like the cicada leaving behind its shell?

Did Mrs. Gandhi understand and throw her love life in the pyre too? Or did she suspect a rival? Or simply follow her husband's lead with spinning?

Does one forget passion? Did she look at herself in the mirror and put away her needs? What could Mrs. Gandhi do when complaint was petty, endurance piety? Take up poetry?

I wonder what Mrs. Gandhi thought when her husband came home and said, *I think it for the best if I had my own bedroom now. Please don't take it personally.*

Cause and effect. Effect and cause. And did Mrs. Gandhi give it another thought because she was after all Mrs. Gandhi, or did she not mention the slight?

Surely, she thought something when alone, when she was lying down in the dark cool of her room. Surely there must've been some resentment gossamer slender. Some sense of her days slipping beyond reach. *I am too young to be old*, Mrs. Gandhi may have thought. She may have claimed this even aloud to herself or to her husband.

But the sarcophagus of celibacy is alabaster and sealed her to her fate. This was not what biographers investigate, nor did Mrs. Gandhi think it apropos to leave behind her personal thoughts.

In the stillness of the night, when cicadas sang with longing, did Mrs. Gandhi listen?

Poem Written at Midnight

I felt so alone
In my marriage
With my husband,
Who was not my husband.

And so I let him go.

I feel so alone
In my city
That is not my city.

And so I hope to flee.

I feel so alone
In my life
That is not my life.

Suéltame, mi vida.
Ya no soy tuya.
Deja de hacerme infeliz.

Year of My Near Death

Six months after
my mother died
a ribbon unspooled
from my uterus
like a stillborn child.

At fifty-three
the womb awoke,
exhaled,
and spoke
one last time.
For my mother's sake,
my own.
I, who birthed
no one in life,
birthed grief.

Thin red line
on a road map
guiding my escape
from servant
to master.
From daughter
to adult ever after.

My body spoke
once before

at thirty-three,
year of my near death,
year of my cross.

I succored despair
with silence, sleep.
Measured self-
worth by others.
A child still
borrowing to pay
the bills. No good
at anything but words.
And what good were words
when the month began?

Nine months the uterus
did not breathe.
Nine months wavered
before the breach.
Saved by Providence,
angels or ancestors.
Stigmata to prove
this story true.

I've died twice and twice
survived. At thirty-three,
the Christ year.
And twin decades later
when my mother
transformed herself
to light.

Twice died.
Twice death-defied.
Marvel at the body's power
to speak, mend, resurrect.
Forgive.

Letter to Pat LittleDog After Losing Her Son

I don't think we can love too much, do you?
I think there is an *ad infinitum* to give
and receive love. And I know as fact
we continue to receive love after
this thin life. I know, not believe,
this is law. Perceived like water
wrinkled by wind. Or,
can't-be-ignored as lightning.

You are a woman who knows the
knowing. I hope your son continues
speaking. And you continue listening.

My father speaks to me
like the wings of a stingray.
My mother shimmers in air,
a silver moth. I know when
they are here. As in life,
different as ever.
One is water.
The other atmosphere.

But what I do
not know in this lifetime,
to love as a mother loves a son.

I want to say as they say here,
I accompany you in your dolor.

Accompany you and all who
carry this wound daily.
I, who birthed no one.

May I give you
the moon as consolation?
May it bring back your boy.
Add his name to the conversation
of light you send and give.
Receive and send. Receive
this love I send tonight, my friend.

Día de los Muertos

On Day of the Dead I ask you to come
home with me to see my altar.
That's a better line than come and see my etchings.

You do come. Like the spirits that night.
You follow the *xempoaxóchitl* petals and make
your way to my door, that door abandoned and
solitary a full year. You make your way and say
you've been sad, and I say I've been sad too,
because it's true, I have.

The one before you
alive and haunting my heart, and I
want and long for release from the hurting.
You come with your own ghost following you.
Save me, we think, but don't say it.

I ask, Thirsty? And serve you *mezcal* before you answer.
Drink the bottle left for *los difuntos*, clink our *copitas*.
I'll send you home with the *cabrito* I set out for my father,
the chocolate *bizcochitos*, the *buñuelos* on a clay plate.
Everything but the confetti jello, I say, and laugh.

Sal y agua on this altar. Salt perhaps for our tears,
water for the dead who are always thirsty.
Scent of warm wax candles and acrid marigolds.
Edith Piaf singing "La vie en rose." Chavela Vargas.
Lola Beltrán. Nina Simone's "I Put a Spell on You."
And I wonder if that *cabrito* will cast its magic spell.

The night is long.
We talk late though you have to get up early.
Talk while the dead come back and savor us. Talk,
which is a kind of *alimento,* a nourishing.
Talk *con ganas,* as they say. You and I.
With feeling.

Buen árbol / A Good Tree

A SONG FOR GUITAR

El que a buen árbol se arrima,
Buena sombra le cobija.
Arrímate. Anímate.
Don't be afraid of me.

If you were smart
You'd know I'm a good good tree.
If you were smart
You'd know I'm a good good tree.

I'm the finial and flag of my own nation.
I'm the school of knocks.
I'm a little bit of comfort mixed
With a little bit of consternation.
I'm the waltz of reason
In the season of rain at last!

If you were smart
You'd know I'm a good good tree.
If you were smart
You'd know I'm a good good tree.

Sweet *huisache*, teach me.
Nourish me, *nogal.*
Alamo, fortify.
Mesquite, endurance please.

I've waited out drought.
Sprouted from my own fire.
Survived the hailstorm
Of desire. Desire.
If you only knew.

If you were smart
You'd know I'm a good good tree.
If you were smart
You'd know I'm a good good tree.

The flower and the fruit am I.
Butterflies breathing life am I.
Resurrection and redemption am I.
Pie in the sky am I.
Kid and wise guy am I.
The still and the gale am I.
Fever and frustration am I.
The evening tide am I.
The soup without the fly am I.
The whole *naranja* am I.

I've died and risen
From the ash of my own
Hesitation. I'm creation.
But you don't see.

If you were smart
You'd know I'm a good good tree.
If you were smart
You'd know I'm a good good tree.

I don't have time for attitude sickness
At this altitude.
I don't have time for percolators,
Nuclear reactors.

I don't need a flash-in-the-pan
Bit of ecstasy
When I've been struck by light.
I'm my own Las Vegas
Night with real stars
For the show. I'm in it
For the mystic. Stick
Around and I'll show you
A thing or two.

I'm a good good tree.
I'm a good good tree.
I'm a good good good
Good tree.

Cisneros

sin

censura

———

Mount Everest

Because he was there.
Back in 1982
—Why not?
was the question.
Not—Why?

What's more,
he was a poet.
Alluring
before I knew
better.

His name?
Ethan. Seamus.
Elton. Or Ian.
Poetry to me.
An empire to conquer.
A foreign language to master.
A notch on my unchastity
belt when my notches
were few.

May I remind you
I was twenty-eight only
in years. My true
age was oak.
Seedling. More

acorn perhaps. Or
possibly spore.

I remember hardly
anything except
he wrote me a poem
when I flew away,
some goodbye,
heartless nothing
is what I recall.

He lived in Old
Town. Hipster
city. A cool I
couldn't afford.
I suffered
neighborhood
envy, apartment
hunger. This
may have been
his true spell,
come to think of it.

But what
I cannot forget.
His bed.

The mattress
crinkled
as if wrapped
in cellophane.

As if stuffed
with Rice Krispies.

I couldn't sleep.
Always.
Left before dawn.
Taxied home.

My futon on
the floor never
more welcoming.

Right now he's
probably
wed to Pippa.
Cosima.
Fiona or Poppy.

Don't remember
much. Some men
are sexier
with their clothes
on. Don't

remember
the sex.
Funny.

Just the mattress.

Variations in White

i.

I am Paracho guitar when you are in me.
Am balsa I am. A harp for wind I am.
A holy thing without a name.
My body a white hum only the leaves can hear.

ii.

There should be a word for this
greed. Your knee
nudging open my knees.

iii.

Because
I cannot take you in my mouth or in my sex,
I ask you to come on my skin.
You dip your fingers in this holy water
I ask you to taste for me.
You do. For me.
You watch me watch you.

iv.

You're a little pearl in my bed, Perlita.
You're a little pearl, Perlita.
Beautiful, pretty.
Perlita, you sleep as I write this.
Perlita, I sleep as you read this.

Eres una perla en mi camita, Perlita.
Eres una perla, Perlita.
Bello, bonito.
Duermes, Perlita, mientras escribo.
Duermo, Perlita, mientras lo lees.

v.

For whose pleasure
a string of saliva
from the lips of the lover
to the beloved's sex.

In My Little Museum of Erotica

In my little museum
of erotica
I would place your feet.

I would place your feet
sandwiching
my feet.

Their softness.
Their heat.

And I would
place your arms
as you do mornings,
beneath my neck,
around my waist,
tugging me towards you,
my back to your chest.

This
well-beingness
I would set
on a Corinthian
column.

And those
who are aesthetes
of mornings and feet
would say, Ah!
Yes!

My Mother and Sex

Eight live births.
How many dead?
Who knew? Not us.
Her seven survivors.

When a bedroom
Scene flashed on TV
She'd shriek and
Scamper to her room,
As if she'd seen
A rat.

It made us laugh. What
Were we? Immaculate
Conceptions? Could be

Sex for her was dead.
A duty dreadful as cooking
For her famished army. Sad
To think this. Pure

Postulation from lack of
Conclusive conversation.
She never talked of sex.

Especially not with me.
She said

I put everything
In a book. Agreed.

But what was worse?
The truth,
Or my imagination?

What I know for sure:
Rapture for her,
A library record symphony.
Ecstasy, opera in the park.

Intimate pleasure,
Books.
Freire, Terkel, Chomsky.
Herculean. Brilliant. Men

Unlike the man who
Shared her bed, who
Favored *Sábado Gigante*
To Sebastião Salgado.

And yet Father spoiled her.
His Mexican empress.
Parícutin tempestuous.
Clueless to what she craved.

Her red flare
Sent up weekends: Help!
There's no intelligent life here!

Evenings in the blue
Moonbeam of TV,
Father mesmerized by
Mexican, thick-thighed floozies—
Mother's word, not mine—
Shaking their hoochie-coochies.

Father never
Drank, ran off, split flesh.
Brought home each faithful
Friday, a paycheck. Why
Would she complain?

She lived alone
In a house full of lives
By the time I knew her.
Snake bitter. Mingy.
Dead before being born.
A woman in formaldehyde.

Stepping on Shit

Sol says, *Buena
fortuna* is on its way.
Money's sure
to arrive today
or next.

Pesos.
Or better yet,
dólares.

A sale
of her labor on canvas
thanks to the new pups
who have littered
the garden with luck.

Her house,
like mine,
the sum of a woman's
life creating.

A flower in a white wimple
sprouted from the organ cacti
yesterday. Today
it furls itself
against the rain.

I'm a witness
in this house of invention.
I write. And watch
myself write.
Furl and unfurl myself
when I shut or open
my laptop.

Sol, success upon
success, good-looking kids,
sweet dollop of a grandchild,
a house ready for its close-up,
and stellar career,
complains.
Sol carries her
one regret like a
dark cloud on a stick—
she's alone.

In the guest house,
I unpack my breasts
from their holsters.
Savor cotton against skin.
Read propped in bed
at leisure. But keep
a sweater within reach.
In case the handyman
barges in.

Look forward to the day
when I'm old enough
to not care.

At sixty-six, not there yet.
At sixty-six I watch the years
gather in the *cenotes* of my eyes,
in the theater drapery of the neck,
and—surprise!—
the dolphin pale underbelly
of my upper arms.

Trickster time arrived
while I slept.
It takes some getting used to.
I watch my transformation
bemused. Just as I once
watched myself alter into
my woman's body. Watch
and marvel now as then.
Relieved to some degree.
Fascinated with where
I am and where I am
traveling.

Poor Sol.
Stranded without a man.

To tell the truth,
I don't want to see
someone my own age
naked. Nor have
him see me.
Nothing to do with
shame or modesty.

More akin to fear
we might laugh.

I read while
the new pups
yap in the garden.

Relieved wherever
my steps take me.

Dólares or *dolores*.

Accept whatever
is on my path.

Naranja completa

i.

Do I miss
Having a man
Enter me?

Crack
Me in two?

Before. After.
I do

Not.
Truth be
Told,

Never.

Am Cavafy
In love
With memory.
Alive with
Story. Do

I miss the
Acapulco rush
Of the dive

Into the fire
Of foam?

The plummeting
Into the sea
Of myself?
Profound mystery?
I do

Not. The
Wound between
My legs taut
As cat gut
On guitar.

An Egyptian
Tomb winched
And looted.

Relieved
To be my own
Destroyer.

I enter my
Body with
A poem slick
With my own
Spit.
Slide and grunt.
A nice, tight fit.

ii.

In my Taipei
Dream
I'm holding

A penis
In my hand.
A scepter.
A wand
Thick as a cop's
Baton.

Hefty warm.
Pulsing.
Definitely
Alive.

A thing
Attached to no one.
All my own.

A weapon to tap
On my palm.
And ask, Now,

What
Do I want

With this?

You Better Not Put Me in a Poem

One had a long curved scimitar like a Turkish moon.

One had a fat *tamale* plug.

One had a baby pacifier.

One had a lightbulb he was proud of.
>It gave me the creeps.
>I can never forget it.
>I could never pick it out in a police line-up.
>Not in a million years.
>Not even with an AK-47 to the side of my
>>head.

One liked to pull it out like a switchblade when least
expected.
>At his mother's.
>Standing in the bathroom, the door open.
>His ma in the kitchen talking on the phone.
>Me on the couch trying to read.
>He thought this was sexy.

One liked to skim *Playboy* magazines when we were making
love.
>I found this humiliating.

One liked to put his hands on his hips like he was Mister Big
Stuff.
>This pissed me off.

One liked to dip his fingers in his semen and lick them.
     He drove me wild.

One slept in my bed but never touched me.
     This was my choice.

One drew a spiral on the envelopes of all his letters.
     Translation: Your back door is mine alone.

One lived with a woman.

One lived alone but refused to let me see where he lived.
     Like a serial killer with something to hide.

One liked to whack me with his dong like a cop's baton.
     He had issues.

One liked to dress me as a boy and take me from behind.
     He had issues.

One was an alcoholic and would go on endless riffs.
     The war.
     The women who left.
     The wife he wouldn't.
     One night he called from a bar and left seventeen
        messages on my machine.
     Did I mention he was an alcoholic?

One never touched the stuff. It made him vomit.
     He was always home.

One drove a nervous car with too many miles and not enough
  insurance.

But every weekend he drove two hundred miles in
frantic traffic to see me.

One never came even when I offered to pay the airfare.

One was married to somebody. A string of somebodies.
We saw each other off and on/in between/during/
above and below/over
A quarter of a century.

When he divorced the last time, I realized finally:
He was the father almighty's approval.
I would never get his approval.
I didn't need his approval anymore.
I had made him up.

When he came, he:
Hiccupped like a dolphin.
Snorted like a horse.
Embarrassed me hollering like a girl.
Was strangely silent like a deer.
Panted like a little dog and planted a kiss on my
butt.

Each and every time.

Never. And afterwards he:
Laughed a little.
Wheezed.
Hacked up a furry cough.
Sprinted off to the shower like I was the plague.
Lit up a smoke.

Never smoked.

Had a collapsed lung.

Had only one lung and was a percussionist.
          After our goodbye I sent him
Pawnshop bongo drums and marshmallows from Texas
          All the way to an address in Athens.
A year later the bongo drums and marshmallows came back
     unopened.
                    Across how many oceans?
A package stamped in Greek letters: "Address Unknown."
          But I read it as: "Undress Alone."

I sent a hundred-dollar bouquet of parrot
          Tulips to a restaurant where one worked as a
               bartender
Even though he was terrible in bed because:
          I was grateful.
          I was needy.
          I was young.
          (See above.)

          I was/am/always will be a romantic.

Which is the same as saying: I fall in love all by myself.

I sent one a poem.
          I never saw him again.

I sent one a twenty-seven-page letter wrapped around a brick
     for dramatic effect.

I sent one postcards from Trieste, Sarajevo, Sparta, Sienna,
   Perpignan,
        Describing my other lovers.
All he did was laugh.

One was a Tejano fitness freak from Austin.
        Tremendous.
        A lottery prize.

        I'm not kidding.

Until he opened his mouth and spoke:
        Like a guitar.
        Like a Texan.
        Like a redneck Texan.
Once when I was making *licuados* for breakfast, he said,
        Great, I love smoothies!

One knew what a woman wants above all else is words.
        To be told he loves her.
        To be told how he is going to love her as he is
          loving her.
        To be told there is no woman like her.

I can't forget him.

I don't remember his name.
        He is not my ex,
        Nor my y, nor even my z.
        He is my *eterno.*

One night on a bed of sand, under a canopy of falling stars,
　　　　　One, who wanted to make love to him,
Made love to me.
　　　　　He to him. I to they.

And afterwards I concluded a ménage à trois is useless
　　because:
　　　　　I need love.
　　　　　A semblance of love at least.
　　　　　Eternity.
And how can you ignite eternity if preoccupied with—*How
　　do I look?*

One didn't care what he looked like, and this was precisely
　　why
　　　　　He was sexy.
　　　　　He was as impeccable and godly as *GQ*.
　　　　　But the more exquisite he grew, the more I turned
　　　　　　　into a rodent.
　　　　　He was my own height and weight.
　　　　　It was easy to flip him over in bed, and the fact
　　　　　　　that I could
　　　　　Made me feel powerful.
　　　　　And I liked this power.

One was big as a redwood, and when he lay on top
　　　　　Of me, I felt like hollering: *Timberrrrrrrrrrr!*

One was violet like the ink from a sea creature, beautiful but
　　deadly.

The skin beneath his clothes glowed from within
    like a lamp of alabaster.
His thing was a blue baby born without air.
His thing was pink like an angry child holding its
    breath.

I don't remember his thing. I don't remember anything.

One confessed, after making love to me, he was still in love
    With a ballerina who had moved away to Kansas.
        Then,
He bought me pancakes.

One confessed he was still in love with an actress he'd
    dumped when
        She was an unknown but was now celebrated in
        Cannes
And Paris. And this was killing him.

One bought me:
    A five-pound typewriter.
    A white Izod polo shirt I never wore because it
      was too Dallas.
    A bag of *pan dulce* and put me to bed as if I was his
      only child.
    But,

I was in love with a sex-*puto* who made
    Love like a water-hose drowning a riot.

One took pictures of me nude when I was too shy to be nude.

I took pictures of me nude when I was too old to be nude.

It was obvious one had an Oedipal complex.
        I was forty. He was twenty-one.

I lost interest in one, because I thought he looked like an old
    man.
        He was forty. I was twenty-eight.

Pee on me, one demanded, and I knew I had to get out of
there.

I came to bed wearing nothing but a belt of bells like a flock
of sheep.

I came to bed wearing nothing but a mink coat.

I came to bed wearing a granny gown and long underwear.

I came to bed the moment one called, because he had to get
    up early and go to work,
        And if I didn't, he said I wasn't going to get
            any.
And his love is the sweetest memory.

We made love on a train in Genoa in a restroom that smelled
    of pee.
        I hated/adored/was terrified of him because:
        I was poor, and worse, ashamed of being poor.
        I knew he would eventually leave me.
        I wanted him to destroy me.

I thought pain was necessary.
I wanted to be him.
(All of the above.)

One was a pre-med student, and after making love would:
Ask me to cough.
Tap on my back.
Thump me like a drum.
Read my body as if I was a well-tuned machine.

I had a crush on one until he appeared at my door
One night with a mustache *exactly* like my
brother's.

I met one in Tenejapa when he rose
From the Mayan jungle like a plumed serpent.

I met one across a boardroom table where he licked my
nipples with his eyes.

I met one at a bar where a gay friend and I both wanted him,
but
I was the only one brave enough to ask,
Are you gay or are you straight?
Silence. *Why?*
Because I don't have a lot of time.

One shook like a little tree when I left him.
There were no tears from me.

I shook like a little tree when one left me.
There were no tears from him.

Subsequently I learned this emotional equation:
>The first one to cry robs the other of the need to.

One was a sham shaman, and when we first made love he
>Smudged me with *copal* and let me place my
>>tongue on his scars.

One became famous, and they make movies about his books.

One is a loser. He teaches at a university where they don't care he's a hustler.

One got married to Hello Kitty, though I suspect he's in the closet.

One was Opus Dei. He dumped me for a Catholic he knocked up.

One wanted to knock me up just so he could say he knocked me up.

One was an anarchist, and I can't forget the sex.

I don't remember the sex. I remember him, and that was sexy enough.

One was bi, and now he's gay.

One was straight, and now he's celibate.

One had teeth like a rat, and now he can afford to have them fixed.

One was in love with a man, and when they kissed each other
    once
                In front of me, slowly, deliberately, a cigarette
                    burning flesh,
I was neither jealous nor sad but
                Fascinated like a fleck of glitter somersaulting
In a globe of snow.

I was Cinderella searching for the perfect fit,
                And when I tried his on for size, I knew.

It was the opposite of childbirth. One was born in my life
                When he slid in with a grunt, and it was then,
                    I knew.

One was soft as a custard cone. I always felt it was my fault.
                Once I dreamt I was carrying his penis through an
                    airport
When, without warning, it sputtered a geyser of shit.
                I rushed it to the ladies'. Hesitated.
Decided the men's room. Then paused.
                I wasn't sure where to go, but one thing I
                    knew.
Over and over I said to aghast bystanders,
                But it's not mine, it's not mine.

You better not, he said kicking
                Off cowboy boots, unzipping his tight
Jeans, *put me in a poem.*

And the arrogance at first
          When I had no such intent. Well,
I just knew

That would be the first,
          If not the last,
Thing I would do.

Woman Seeks Her Own Company

Profession:
Word weaver.

Fervent believer:
Humanity of humanity.

Proclivity:
Daydreaming.

Hobby:
Night-dreaming.

Sensitivity:
Everything.

Pleasure:
Books.
Biographies and poetry especially.
Lessons on how to mitigate disaster.

Medications:
Pen and paper.

Purpose:
Preservation.

Leisure:
Home.

Alone.
Unstressed.
Uncombed.
Undressed.

Indulgences:
Movies.
Pre-Hays and
Italian tragedies.
Because a good cry
Balances out a good laugh.

Favorite actress:
Anna Magnani.

Preferred company:
Burros.
Elephants.
Clouds.

Favorite soundtracks:
Trees speaking wind.
Rain.
Night thunder.

Nagual:
Ocelotl.
Like a *lotl.*

Nemeses:
Rodents.

Automobiles.
Planes.

Savored scents:
Mother's lilies of the valley.
Grant Park lilacs.
Abuelito's cigar.
México in the morning.

Family:
Friends.

Strangers:
Kin.

Achilles' heel:
Rescuing.

Vulnerabilities:
Six brothers.

Anathema:
Babies.
Math.

Best trait:
Generosity.

Fatal flaw:
Generosity.

Put to rest:
Saber repartee and
Molotov bon mot.

Luxury:
Seclusion.

Foibles:
Love life.

Merit:
My life as witness.

Height:
5'2" or 157.48 cm last measured.
Diminishing with age.
However, simultaneously
Growing in self-worth.

Weight:
Done being concerned.
Shapeshifting into
Chichén Itzá.

Relinquished:
Vanity of paint.

Ever passionate:
Fashion.

Personal aim:
Mystic. This
Lifetime or next.

Auto-criticism:
At peace with being
Work-in-progress.

Solo-amusement:
Laughs aloud
At her own jokes.

Encourages:
Eccentricities.

Dislikes:
Chit-chat.
Parsimony.
Satellite loyalties.

Fond of:
Xolos.
Magueys.
Peonies.

Different drummer:
Since birth.
Path not taken.
All that.

Culinary skills:
None.

Decadences:
Unmade bed.
Weekends.
Some weekdays too.

Recompense:
Lounging like an odalisque.

Preferences:
What others think
Sent to department
Of dearly departed.

Artistry:
At sixty-five convinced
Just getting started.

Pilón

When in Doubt

When in doubt,
Wear faux leopard.

When in doubt,
Err on the side of generosity.

When in doubt,
Greet everyone as you would the Buddha.

When in doubt,
Collect blessings from those who own nothing.

When in doubt,
Absorb biographies to avoid life's major mistakes.

When in doubt,
Make life's major mistakes.

When in doubt,
Pay attention to the vendor shouting *"Diooooos,"*
Even when you find out he was only shouting *"Gaaaaas."*

When in doubt,
Carry a handkerchief *and* a fan.

When in doubt,
Thank everyone. Twice.

When in doubt,
Heed the clouds.

When in doubt,
Sleep on it.

When in doubt,
Treat all sentient and insentient beings as kin.

When in doubt,
Forgive us our myopia
As we forgive those who are myopic against us.

When in doubt,
Unreel your grief to a tree.

When in doubt,
Remember this.
We are all on a
Caucus-race.

There is no start.
No finish.
Everyone wins.